The Boy With No Face

The Boy With No Face

KEVIN HIGGINS

salmonpoetry

Published in 2005 by
Salmon Publishing,
Cliffs of Moher, County Clare, Ireland
Website: www.salmonpoetry.com
email: info@salmonpoetry.com

ISBN 1 903392 44 6

Cover artwork: Aoife Casby
Cover design & typesetting: Siobhán Hutson

*Salmon Publishing gratefully acknowledges the financial support
of The Arts Council / An Chomhairle Ealaíon*

for Susan

Acknowledgments

Acknowledgments are due to the following magazines, chapbooks and anthologies in which some of these poems first appeared:

The Shop, Orbis, Metre, Fortnight, Paris/Atlantic (France), *The Sunday Tribune, West 47, The Interpreter's House, Psychopoetica, Rattapallax* (New York), *Potpourri* (Kansas), *Gargoyle* (Virginia), *River King Poetry Supplement* (Illinois), *Vallum* (Canada), *Citizen 32, Poems for Lord Hutton, Books Ireland, ROPES, Poetry Ireland Review, The Limerick Leader, www.nthposition.com, Literati Magazine* (online), *www.rattapallax.com/fusebox, Wildeside, The Stinging Fly, Riposte, The Brobdingnagian Times, Poetry Nottingham International, The Heart of Kerry* anthology (Doghouse), *Oasis, The Journal, Listening To The Birth Of Crystals, Fresh* (New Zealand), *Podium 2, Labour of Love* (Canada), *Braquemard, The Red Poets Society, Flaming Arrows, Reality, Asylum, Markings, Weyfarers, The Chancer, The Blue Collar Review* (Virginia), *glór achadh mór, Iota, The Burning Bush, The Apostasy Mag, Poetry Monthly, The Cúirt Journal, Red Lamp, Peace and Freedom, The Coffee House, Muc Mhór Dhubh, Times New Roman, The New Writer, The Galway Advertiser, Crannóg, Aphrodisiac Jacket, From Berlin to Salthill, Blackhole and other poems, 100 Poets Against The War* (Salt Publishing), *Irish Writers Against War* (The O'Brien Press), *Short Fuse: The Global Anthology of New Fusion Poetry* (Rattapallax Press), *In The Criminal's Cabinet* (nthposition), and *Breaking The Skin: New Irish Poetry* (Black Mountain Press).

"Blackhole" won the 2003 Poetry Grand Slam at the Cúirt International Festival of Literature.

"Knives" & "Letter To A Friend About Girls" have been broadcast of RTÉ's *Rattlebag*, "The Boy With No Face" on *The Galway Bay FM Arts Show*, and "Talking With The Cat About World Domination The Day George W. Bush Almost Choked On A Pretzel" on Resonance 104.4 FM (London): *Poems for George W. Bush*.

Contents

Confetti

No-one gets to glimpse a finished canvas,
nor views the film in its uncut entirety.
Too much, too much, to lay it all out
across a pure white sheet on a clean spring noon
all in order and accounted for.
Instead it's all bits and pieces.
Hidden here. Filed away there.
Where no-one would think to look.
Appropriate fragments are carefully chosen
and juggled for appropriate pairs of eyes.
There are hints. The occasional chink.
At twilight, perhaps at dawn, in dimly lit rooms.
They fall like confetti to the floor.
Until, some day, you're there again in that hallway,
where solitude casts the blackest of shadows,
and it all comes out, coheres, like a flaw
yawning sharply across a bare space.

To Hell And Back Again

Now that, at last,
you seem to have found yourself
you often long to be lost again,
to drift down a throbbing street
in the thick of the afternoon
at the centre of your own solar system,
to shillyshally for hours
over a mug of tea and a slice of toast
in some greasy-spoon,
where no-one would even dream
of asking for a cappuccino or a latté,
or, better still, not to bother
leaving your filthy flat all day at all,
but, when the last ray of sun has, finally, gone away,
to shamble down to the kebab house
for a pickled onion and a portion of chips
because you don't have the cash
to use the brothel around the back.
But if you slip from these shackles,
your future which opens up
like a new continent that, of course,
must be conquered,
this clean living which sometimes
fits you like a collar and tie on a boiling hot day
at one of those awkward family occasions,
if you go back to all that liberty, to all that Hell,
you might not make it back again this time.

Knives

It wasn't from the wind I took it:
with a grandad who once threatened
to tie a cat across the hedge,
so that nosy bastard neighbours, as they passed,
would gawk at it instead of in at him;
and a father who often likened
Albert Reynolds' face to a torn slipper;
I come from a long line of men,
who saw words not as decorations
but weapons, knives with which to cut
others down to size.

By Five o'clock

Your last day at the office gone down the drain,
you're null and void once again.
On Quay Street nothing but loud-mouthed money.
You live in a city—no a country—
run by idiots you went to school with.
Your father'd put his finger
precisely where you've gone wrong,
if he wasn't off in a mobile home
with her from number five.
But, in a week or so,
the up-side of idleness will strike you.
A universe of time for nothing but writing!
Your satires will suffer as you run out of characters
on a thin diet of teletext news.
Your girlfriend will dump you.
(Your lover won't phone.)
The blonde in the bookshop won't laugh at your jokes.
You'll visit your mother more and more often,
become what the girls at the office
call "the Norman Bates sort". Look in the mirror!
The smirk has slipped, Sunny Jim.
The face on the floor is definitely yours.

In The Cold Light Of Day

When you examine the scum in your favourite mug,
and look at the cut of your three day stubble;
your underwear so threadbare it's barely even there;
when, to quote a million rejections slips,
"Your work could be much more technically crisp";
when you have all of this, and so much more,
it's obvious the fact you've just been sacked
is simply a blip in an otherwise glittering career.

To certain lyric poets

This lyric poet sees
his own reflection everywhere.
Even, 'her hair on the pillow
like freshly fallen snow',
is there to let us know
he still gets laid,
although, in this case,
she probably passed
through Robert Graves's hands first.
But we should be gentle
when we mention
"the narrowness of his range",
that lovely little phrase the critics invented,
a device to side-step saying, instead,
"he only ever talks about himself".
Every poem is another love-letter
to the person to whom
his whole life's work
has been dedicated.
He's been known
to agonise for hours
over a single word
and each one of them
is precisely meant
because, to him,
words are beautiful things,
flowers to be arranged
around an altar to his ego.

I am Ireland

after Pádraic Pearse

I am Ireland:
I am the love-child of Brian Keenan and John Waters.
I drive Lebanese terrorists and Sinéad O'Connor bonkers.
I will go on forever.

Great my glory:
I am Enya's next album
and Michael Flatley's other testicle rolled into one.

Great my shame:
I am Frank McCourt's next book
and, even worse, I'm his brother.

I am Ireland:
I am Louis Walsh waiting for the Milli Vanilli to hit the fan.
I keep a hyena in my front garden and I am ready!

President Robinson Pays Homage to Lord Haw Haw, 21 October 1996

after Paul Durcan and Francis Stuart

On the stroke of midnight,
during a secret ceremony in Arás an Uachtaráin,
President Robinson placed the Collar of Gold
around the neck of Lord Haw Haw
(the broadcaster formerly known as William Joyce)
"It's a comfortable fit",
Galway's most famous bag of bones was heard to remark.
Paying her homage to Haw Haw,
speaking stridently and without a script,
just like Haw Haw himself used to do in the old days,
Mrs Robinson stated that when her own thinking
had been making its shapes, Haw Haw's example
had proved invaluable.
It taught her the crucial role of the individual in history.
"His is an awkward, an uncomfortable voice."
In response, Haw Haw, after bowing to the President,
stated that, as a citizen of The City of The Tribes,
he felt honoured and proud.
A relaxed President relaxing at his side, posed for photographs
with the skeleton of the legendary broadcaster.

A Postcard from Minneapolis

"Lots of ghosts, cars and junk
but strangely little history
here in old America..." And then swiftly on
to all your favourite whinges.
"Don't wanna be here. Don't even drink beer..."

But as your card to me shot
postmarked from the machine
—September 10th 21.53—an alarm-clock
somewhere was being well and truly set.
Luggage. Tickets. Everything ready. A man
muttering something in Arabic. And soon
floating in from a neighbouring room:
'This is the ten o'clock news.'

Then from Greenwich Village to San Diego
the streets slowly emptying, until
—everything standing momentarily still—
America's a movie set, with actors
everywhere waiting for the man
to shout: 'Lights. Camera. Action!'

Winter in Minnesota

Forty seven next November. He's almost as over
as Hubert Humphrey's White House hopes.
Never imagined he'd have to winter back in Minnesota,
be there standing on his mother's front lawn,
like a distant cousin in a photograph no-one remembers taking.
The Dylan Thomas of Minneapolis; got so caught
up with mythmaking and pool-hall brawls,
twenty five years later he isn't even Garrison Keillor;
will settle for the woman, who'll aid and abet him
through the next bottle of whiskey, and maybe
tend the grass, the daisies when he's done.

Exclamation Mark

He's the sort of American,
who'd go meekly, quoting Wallace Stevens,
all the way to the electric-chair;
an exclamation mark, where his face used to be.

Our Resident Expert

If only the listeners knew,
that our resident expert
who now waxes lyrical
about declining standards,
is the same guy, who,
back in 1985, wore ankle-boots
and imagined he was Bono.
"Walk away, walk away. I will follow."
And, at five foot nothing,
the growth hormone having
apparently forgotten him,
he was forever trying to pull,
someone's sister's standards
down around her ankles.

The Satirist

Society may flash its knickers at him,
but flowers or love songs, he will not bring them.
Instead the audience ripples with nervous laughter
as, from his jacket, he takes a scalpel.
And, his mask slipping just a little,
they see him briefly as he really is:
coming with a warrant, all their names on it.

The Shop Street Crooner

A hard-luck story which goes on forever,
with a voice that certainly carries;
he rattles eardrums all day long.
He fought for Ireland and the mice
were squealing in his prison cell. He can't
go on with these suspicious minds.
(He's everyone's Uncle Willie
at that wedding in Crossmolina.)
But how did it come to this?

The regular flutter, the occasional binge;
he was always on the throne,
poring over the racing pages;
waiting for the big winner to come,
the way pilgrims in Rome
wait for white smoke.
Very much his own man:
a great one for folding the arms;
he was second to none at backing certainties,
which fell at the last, or lost by a nose,
in the three fifteen at Chepstow.
You can still see the print
of his ex-wife's shoe on his derriére.

Café Du Journal

"I feel like a European."
"I know what you mean",
the Czech waitress tells him,
and then just stands there,
dazzled by the headlights
of his Andy Williams smile,
as he eyes up every square inch
of her autonomous republic:
from the Bohemia of her behind
to the Prague Spring of her cleavage:
in that oh so casual 'I only want
the Sudetenland' manner of his.

The Libertine

Plagued with infections, vice has its price,
he just passes them on, like good advice.

Shirtless in Shop Street boxing the invisible man on a Saturday afternoon

How you love to drone about non-events,
which like blank jigsaw pieces, soggy old cardboard,
always add up to nothing. If anyone were to fall
for your personal myth, they'd know
your woes are just the worst, like
Tuesday evening's young Canadian
in Taylor's Bar, who wouldn't stoop
to grant you the pleasure of tickling her fancy,
and when you suggested you should rub
your bald head between what you imagined might be
her attentive breasts, she didn't even have the courtesy
to make her excuses, but just upped, left you stranded,
another Tuesday evening high and dry,
stumbling around a corner in a few hours time,
legless around another towards a possible black-eye.

    She could have given you the benefit
of the non-existent doubt and the chance
to paw her tight-lipped thighs
one last time. The situation forced your hand,
you had to stay til closing-time
and go back last night for an encore,
until that ape of a bar-man manhandled you out the door,
and now you're down to just loose change.

    And how you ended up in such an invidious position
is one of life's great big mysteries, as you ask me
for yet another fiver. But you've a distance yet to travel
before you fall to the level of the guy,
who as I speak, this busy Saturday afternoon,
is naked from the waist up and throwing
cockeyed punches at an invisible opponent
on the pavement across the road.

He gave the invisible man a good left jab
as I handed you that fiver, which now,
like his shirt, is another lost cause. Yes, my friend,
though you've a distance yet to travel
before you reach his shirtless in Shop Street
boxing the invisible man on a Saturday afternoon level,
that distance is less and, then again, even less,
until one day the only question left,
when we meet on Shop Street, will be,
well then, old boy, whatever became of your shirt?
Whatever became of your shirt?

A real Galwegian

Because when you watch the woman
sitting next to you writing an e-mail
in what looks like Korean, or find yourself asking
someone called Candy from Saskatchewan
for two bagels with cream-cheese,

it occasionally still hits you; how it's
like the blink of an eyelid since, down this street,
the coffee was rotten, and a night out
just a pint of sad *Smithwicks* eventually
emerging in a withered hand
from a back-street hatch, a barman telling

a complaining Yank how the lock broken
on that toilet door has been that way
for nearly twenty years, and not
a single shit stolen yet.

The Leader

He's coming and will give no advance warning
but kick the door down at four in the morning
or whenever it suits him—*it's his country*—
and be halfway up the stairs before you see him there.
He'll hit you with a killer smile
and a million grudges bound together in one big fist.
His name will not be Haider (or anything like that)
but something with an altogether more familiar ring to it.
He's the sort of man who hasn't read
Mein Kampf just yet. But he'll be here,
like the old man buying *The Racing Post*
who growls about 'invaders' or the skinhead
with the petrol bomb whose hour is striking now.

Desperate Weather

If it wasn't Linz, 1906,
but here and now, there he'd sit,
huddled at a table in *Le Graal*,
a same time, same place, most nights,
usual table type of guy,
to whom you'd maybe nod
or mutter something, here so often,
you can't but know him,
an edge of the picture
all night wind-bag sort of character,
his audience of one typically far
more taken with the waitress's arse.
Nothing to his name, which somehow slips you,
but a lottery ticket and a date with FÁS.
The best parts of most days, he snores them away,
late afternoon catches him
with paints and canvas, *a budding genius*,
a derivative style all of his own.
And, Lord preserve us, he writes "poetry",
is influenced by Wagner but mostly Mother.
His usual table sometimes taken. "It's okay if I sit here?
The name's Hitler." "You look familiar."
"Isn't it desperate weather." "Yes, desperate weather."

The Voice Of Reason

He wants to keep you talking
about the gold he's seen in those Romanian teeth,
while they sneak Liam Lawlor out the back door.
Whatever the 'equality brigade' might say,
the dogs in the street know that gold
does not belong in teeth such as those,
but should be siphoned away Ansbacher style.
He only met Frank Dunlop once or twice,
is the innocent victim of a campaign of lies
by clever Nigerians armed with PhDs;
will do any gymnastics necessary to hide
the cut-throat razor he has behind his back,
until the time is ripe and it's one minute to midnight.

The Hidden Hand

'the hidden hand of the free market'
    —Nigel Lawson, Chancellor of the Exchequer 1983-89

I'm omnipresent, a bit like God,
but the difference is, I exist.
I live in your alarm-clock made in Quandong,
in the paper this is written on.
I set the interest rate, decide the price.
I believe in Milton Friedman
and he believes in me. I sometimes
work in mysterious ways; can
make a billion bucks vanish
just like that. I made Joseph Kennedy rich,
tossed Robert Maxwell off his yacht.
I am the be all, the end all; the hidden hand
which makes you dance.

The FÁS Man Cometh

I've come to my senses
(or so everyone says)
and have finally mastered
the subtle art of bending over.
And sure enough, I've found it's true,
reality can be adjusted
if you assume the correct posture.
In my new position,
as an apparatchik of the New Irish Order,
I assist the work-shy
in overcoming their shyness.
(I'm the example I use to prove
the treatment works, as soon they will too.)
No pain no gain, or put another way,
if it isn't hurting it isn't working.
When I'm finished with them
they'll be in a position
to make realistic life decisions as well.
Old mind-sets must be set aside.
Labour In Irish History? I've left it behind.
And as for *The Internationale?*
I've managed to forget every last word.
My boss is less impressed
by anything I've learnt
than with the extent of my amnesia.
Society has finally given me a role, a mobile phone
and an electronic gadget which can tell
the time in Adelaide and Tokyo,
everything I need to know.
And I'd draw the marrow
from the bones of the idle, undeserving poor
if Mary Harney's department
faxed me a memo to that effect.
The 'I' of THE TIGER.
I want to make it mine.
Yes, MINE! MINE! MINE!

A Brief History of Those Who Made Their Point Politely And Then Went Home

On this day of tear-gas in Seoul
and windows broken at *Dickins & Jones*,
I can't help wondering why a history
of those, who made their point politely
and then went home, has never been written.

Those who, in the heat of the moment,
never dislodged a policeman's helmet,
never blocked the traffic or held the country to ransom.
Someone should ask them: "Was it all worth it?"

All those proud men and women, who never
had the National Guard sent in against them;
who left everything exactly as they found it,
without adding as much as a scratch to the paintwork;
who no-one bothered asking: "Are you or have you ever been?",
because we all knew damn well they never ever were.

Talking With The Cat About World Domination The Day George W. Bush Almost Choked On A Pretzel

Now that pretzel's gone and done
something an expert like you never would
—loosening its hold a split-second too soon—
I think it's time we revised our strategy.
Just sitting back waiting for the big collapse?
Face facts. It isn't happening.
If there's a job to be done, why not us?

This time tomorrow we'll be in Washington
telling Bush to come out with his hands up.
Faced with me and you, Puss, I bet he'll just crumble.
And we'll whisk him off to Guantanamo Bay
where he'll share a cage with the Emir of Kuwait.

I see from the frown wrinkling your brow,
you're worried, perhaps, how
Mariah Carey fans everywhere might react.
Too late for all that. To put it in terms
I think you'll understand: after the years wasted
here in this litter-tray, it's time to deliver
for me and you, Puss. Our battle-cry?
Something snappy? Like?
Yes, I have it! Repeat after me:
Don't make me angry, Mr Magee.
You wouldn't like me when I'm angry.

Else

However hard I try
I just can't shake this defeated feeling,
fallen into such an utter disarray,
I'm a cheek with no smack on it,
a white sheet with no KKK in it,
a page of pornography
and not a single confirmed sighting of an arse in the bare,
or anything better for that or any other matter.
I must have gone to a wrong place with a wrong clock,
like a guillotine with no neck in it,
a leopard-skin with no slapper in it,
I'm a wrong thing wandered into an erroneous context,
a punch with no face waiting to meet it at the other end,
all I can do only is to continue now
and be one own half of something completely else.

A Balancing Act

Consider less the cruel universe,
than the face in the mirror
who always nicks himself shaving;
the bit of a chancer, who's just glad to be here,
given the odds against him
ever having been born were overwhelming.
No Olivier playing Hamlet;
but a B-movie actor who still
can't quite believe the part is his.

You who've come to understand
dialectical materialism like the back of your hand:
your ideas as clinical as surgical instruments:
must know knowledge is a commodity
all too often squandered, that the trick
is not to spot the flaw in every fabric;
to conduct elaborate experiments
in new forms of paralysis.

So what if, like Shakespeare,
you sometimes mix your metaphors.
Leave what they call 'perfection'
to the long-faced followers
of St. John of the Cross.
Never settle for a nil–nil draw.
If life is a sort of a balancing act,
the most careful of men
fall off in the end.

The Red Shoes

"Well tell me this then.
What is it precisely you yearn for in life?
To live? Surely not merely to live...?"

"Oh, no!", her slender frame shook,
as she rushed to interrupt,
"But to dance. Yes, to dance."

"Well if that's the case", he laid it down
detaining her in the coldest of gazes,
"I'll mould you into the greatest dancer who's ever graced
across the stage of the ballet. From such humble origins
could come a phenomenon whose legacy would live on,
while the bland traces which mere mortals—such as these!—
might leave will certainly fade. The shadow you could throw!
Oh, well you know!"

And so she danced.
Through each and every role she swept a breathing flame,
until her fickle human frame desired at least some slight refrain,
a haven into which she might lapse, drowse.
But, though she pleaded that they cease,
the shoes refused her urgent appeals.
From the ephemera of love, the transience of simple being,
from all base passions and other tedious concerns,
they made her dance away.

I can't help puzzling now, as the film concludes,
if a similar fate might have befallen
the Degas girl in green chiffon?
Her eternal dance illuminates the room
from the picture which sits beside the television.

Poetry, I suppose, is my dance.
This pen, no spade to me, but shoes. Like those.
For better and worse, in this I've invested my last
as I strain to rescue some relic at least
from the eraser of life's mere span,
the dwindle of memory's mere recall.

So don't ask me, please, to choose,
between you and these Red Shoes.

January

for Susan

The ashtrays need emptying
and the cat's been sick.
The mice in the attic are giving out stink.
As we watch our breath drift
across the kitchen, central heating
is a luxury as distant as trays
of oysters at the Galway Races.
The year struggles to its feet,
like a lamb stranded in deep snow.
Strange then to think, this evening in Siberia,
that these are the good old days;
I, the unknown "poet and critic",
you, the next F. Scott Fitzgerald,
up all night, putting the world to wrong;
writing new versions of old songs.

Some Cold Water Morning

As downstairs the old man fades,
our days here seem suddenly numbered.
In a matter of months the developers will come
and throw all of this—these rooms
where MacNeice and Mayakovsky
came back to life—into a great big skip, as we
make way for solid types
with planning permission for wives.

The future is as enigmatic as ever,
as unpredictable as the price
of oil in two thousand and twenty,
        but, terrible to think, that we might
one day wake and find
the last of the poetry drained from life,
be stuck there, some cold water morning,
glancing endlessly back as the door finally
shuts on all the great times.

Other People's Rubbish

Now we've dispensed with the diplomacy
and are left, only, with the megaphone,
our voices sound suddenly like white noise
and the room is full of other people's rubbish.
We should have taken this squabble
by the scruff of the neck, let silence throttle it;
got back to that place where 'other people' end
and we begin, before it was too late: to that very first evening,
when, with Joni Mitchell and Wallace Stevens,
and me opening that bottle of plonk,
we filled this room with altogether sweeter sounds than these.

The Slow Revenge

Not the walking question mark you were,
as life delivers its verdict.
Your much-vaunted independence
crumbled as suddenly as the Soviet Union.
Your list of other women: the endless
not known at this address of a trail gone cold.
Already wearing the lines of the coming decline,
you'll soon be whingeing for wedding bells,
because on clear nights you're wide awake
with the knowledge, that the world gets
its slow revenge on single men
in upstairs flats: the terror of turning fifty
with that black and white TV, pictures like this
make you to cling her: the irritating habit
no-one else would have.

Finis

Our train terminating here.
Its doors opening with a string
of anti-climactic clicks, as if a trigger
was being repeatedly squeezed,
when the pistol had already been emptied
into a victim now in no fit state to rebut accusation
after accusation with anything else but blood.

The ammunition we'd stockpiled
for the next inevitable confrontation
is at once as redundant as the sentiments
in the cards on the mantel-piece.
Birthday. Valentines. One to mark the truce
after that penultimate spat of ours.

Your books and other bits and pieces
will, of course, be returned because love,
being human, needs its rituals
and here comes the funeral,
slow as Albinoni's *Adagio in G minor*
and awful as the squall which descends
this evening: November 4th 1999.

The requiem plays, though not for us

Let's never gaze at each other
across an unbridgeable space,
(even through cold panes of glass
 may our fingers reach and touch)
nor battle, separated,
through the mobs of shoppers
and the caustic weather
of a raw November thoroughfare.
May the music we make
be a Spanish guitar,
let no disconsolate adagio
be any creation of ours
and if, of an evening,
you happen to catch me listening
to Mozart's requiem,
it won't be our union
that sombre music
will be mourning.

The Crossroads

I waited at the crossroads,
when only a sprinkle of pink
across the branches
of the Cherry Blossom
hinted the winter was, at last,
slipping into remission,
and until the final yellow
of the Laburnum had flaked
across then burnt grass,
I waited at the crossroads.

Estrangement: A Sequence

1. Till Agony Do Us Part

Just another suburban marriage,
it detonated and toppled in upon itself
raising a frenetic smog of terminal
dust over the migraine sky.

Everyone saw it coming
after it had gone.

If it had a voice it would sound
like ghastly fingernails scraping
all the way down and across
the length and the breadth
of a shrieking blackboard.

2. She Looked Up

Looking up from the kitchen table,
her face withered with impressions of torn pictures,
faded photographs, archaic Christmas cards,
she eyeballed the mist on the window.

The poker faced clouds
had finally broken down.

A lonely pot of tea,
past its best,
kept her company.
They were meant for each other.

3. 3.19 A.M.

There are ashes in the grate at this empty hour of the morning,
and unwashed plates fill the careless kitchen sink,
where the drip of the tap, it still insists.

The Traces of The Silver Sand

for my mother

1. Maine 1963

In nineteen sixties black and white,
from a photograph, you smile.
In a playful pose, as with a friend you strolled
kicking silver sand with such nimble feet
all along that beach where the brilliant sea
so placidly lapped.

2. Galway 1997.

Another year,
it slips through the perpetual hands
of my particular clock. As I turn thirty.
And go on turning. To spin inexorably away.
And these aching eyes, they can't recognise
the blithe smile of bliss that portrait claims
you once wore about your lips.

3. Epilogue

Now American girls sway about your place,
vivid flowers frisk the air for fresh satin kisses.
They snap the hush which would hang around an idle house,
for now your wearying brood, we've all flown.
And these skittish girls to you are not
mere students paying rent.
In the fizzling pools of their wide eyes
you can catch far-flung traces of that silver sand
from along the beach where the brilliant sea
so placidly once lapped.

Families And How To Survive Them

The last shutter now fastened down.
All that remains to be seen
is who'll be first across the Rubicon?
The shouting tired of the sound of itself;
as if an audience is anticipating the first act of attrition,
that one, in and of itself, incidental event,
which will step forward and tear open
the labyrinth we've woven from those necessary lies,
those words best left unspoken.
And when it comes—any moment now—
it'll finish off that final shoddy compromise,
which recent events have fatally undermined.

But why should anyone be forced to listen
to another version of this awful old song?
The racket family history gives off
as it rehashes itself, then as tragedy, now as farce.
Peace now become another lost cause,
if this is war, why not keep it a cold one,
less Bosnia more the Berlin Wall?
We could eye each other at weddings and funerals
from either side of Checkpoint-Charlie,
until one of the latter puts a stop to this nonsense.
But, in the mean time, poison of sort we possess
is best kept bottled and, where necessary, frozen.

Almost Invisible

When winter's chill and pallid spectre
ripples across the horizon
to thrust itself once more
upon a gilded autumn's final fling,
and to roughly wrap dead hands around
the sultry traces of those lingering summer days,

    the rust-red leaves in swollen gardens,
    the buoyant banter of candent girls,
    who pulsed the wild streets
    aggravating the symptoms,

then he will, again, venture from his shady hollow
to hang on the frigid corners of unfrequented lanes
thickly stained in the jet-black of dusk. Almost invisible.

November

November rampages down the avenue,
like a gang of victorious soldiers,
drunk but still thirsting for more,
eager now the slaughter comes easy.

And Winter's bare face glares
everywhere at us. The balding trees,
all along the street, suddenly synchronise
their watches, and admit defeat.

The Evidence

On a narrow lane
which wound to the sea,
I blundered across her locket and chain,
with broken links indicating
it had been torn from her soft throat.
As I fondled it there,
between finger and thumb,
it seemed to whimper.

And her skin, it was the colour
of terror in the whites of the eyes.

Fifty yards further down,
some dark fistfuls of hair,
the same tint she'd put in
that very afternoon,
though the persistence of the drizzle
had made the colour run a little.

And her skin, it was the colour
of terror in the whites of the eyes.

Then by the edge of that lonely shore,
as plain as this day through which these black winds blow,
a small rock bluntly stamped with an immaculate blood-stain.

And her skin, it was the colour
of terror in the whites of the eyes.

No More Tears

Through the increasing murk of the evening,
This Blackness, it slants across our path again.
Not the utter form of sky between stars
but the low sort, a rot which will nag like cancer,
then, suddenly, be nearly everywhere.

And I, Charon, awful old miser,
lurk among black poplars
to snatch the coins
from beneath dead tongues and laugh!
Oh my shaking hands!

Now all is still again.
Laments might pierce the air,
but no, not a syllable packaged away in a mutter
let alone cried out. I, who have no tears.

5.15 a.m.

Insomnia comes like the secret police,
drags you off to a place,
where even the mildew
by the window looks accusingly at you,
until suddenly there he stands:
the Grand Inquisitor. And as he brings
his witnesses filing in, his horrible laugh
says he has all the answers,
the guilty secrets, the lists of names...
In a few hours time you'll embellish everything
with Cherry Blossoms again,
but here and now there's no way out
as he hands you a picture
of a black-hearted bastard,
the man without the mask.

Untitled

Like balls across a snooker table,
the crowd on Shop Street breaks,
as a sudden downpour slaps its face.

Absent Without Leave

A.W.O.L at eleven a.m.
The girl in the plaid school-skirt stands in a shop doorway.
A seductive cigarette dangles from her lips
As she shelters from the lucky rain
Whose promiscuous tongue at least
Got to tenderly stroke the back of her neck.

Letter to a Friend about Girls

after Philip Larkin

What losers we were when it came to girls.
'Pull up to my bumper baby, drive it in between'
played soundtrack to the wet dreams
of small, inconsequential fellas, the likes of us.
And we're talking small on an almost monumental scale.
In duffel coats and awful glasses
we shuffled around the edges of other people's parties
all through the eighties,
gawking down in the general direction
of our stupid, stupid shoes.
If charisma could be distilled,
ours would have been measured
in somewhat less than millilitres.
So small, we barely existed.

On the rare occasions when opportunity
—the tastiest variety—put herself there
to be availed of and there was nothing for it
but to press the advantage all the way home,
we either failed to spot the most obvious signals
—our radar were useless at picking incoming aircraft up—
or else managed to inexplicably miss.
She grinned through the worst jokes
and was clearly prepared to overlook that duffel coat,
but the score on the board stubbornly somehow stayed zero.
The goal could be yawning wide open
and still the ball would either trickle
pathetically wide or go sailing miles over.
And just what exactly were we supposed to say
as another cut-price night at *The Oasis* declined
(with no bachelor flat to which she might be lured back)?
"Let's explore the universe with my last fifty pence piece.
If I empty my pockets perhaps I could stretch as far as a kebab."

1999–1977

I hesitate on Eglinton Street which is as empty as the Cathedral
when the mass had ended and they'd gone in peace.
But this truce which lulls down onto each square inch of this,
the last Sunday in September, doesn't take me in.
Tomorrow the cacophony will rear up again.
Unmistakable school bells will tear the morning in two.
It's as if I'm ten years old and back there in fourth class
without a jot of homework done as usual, heading for
    serious trouble
first thing in the morning. *Caoimhín Ó hUiginn!* Anseo.
To be plucked from the class and sarcastically slung
out into that corridor with its dreary rattles
was even worse than the thought of Mr Greaney's bamboo stick
in 1977 when Galway footballers were always useless as usual
and it rained when they lost and it rained when they lost.

Remembering the Leaving Cert

At times like this; the black
thoughts gathering like jackdaws;
it's as if, after all these years,
I'm still the same schoolboy revolutionary,
who'd rather declare war on the free world,
than swot for an honours maths exam.
There I am, still dreading that moment,
when the supervisor says: "You may begin";
still slouching down St. Mary's Road
the night before the results arrived,
still hoping against hope the envelope
somehow gets lost in the post.

No Such Republic

Socialism, like the buses, is running late.
Your days as an agent of Goldstein finally over;
you're no longer a danger to NATO expansion
or Alan Greenspan's latest plan.
The Secret Police leave you in peace.
And you always pictured an ice-pick
or a Czarist Prison at least;
something more than simply
being crossed off the wanted list;
exiled to that country where resistance
is a thing of the past:
where, when you tell them
where you're from, neighbours snigger
and say, "But, *Comrade*,
no such Republic ever existed!"

The Bankrupt Years

Here we are in the Bankrupt Years, when blood is sluggish
    in the veins,
the streets have been cleared of unmanned barricades
and we are left with only empty gestures to be made.

The curtain is raised over a vacant stage
upon which no more great parts are played,
then down those drapes slump again to shroud this naked scene
and in repeat performance, merely going through the routine,
we have another review of the deserted vacuum that is here.

There are no pieces to be put back in place again,
only the ashes of history falling through fingers.

A blanket of blind fog gives camouflage
to the blatant blather of knaves and bunkum from numbskulls.
Their minds are so open that nothing stays there.

All that seems to be left is to throw a shrug of the shoulders
to the trend of the times and to trudge,
through this desolate cackle, on out of my age.

Nostalgia, 1990

A miscellany of recollections,
trinkets tossed from a deep black sea
teasing to the verge of being again.
The particular stale smoke whiff of the Northern Line.
Morden—14 minutes.
Hanging around for a 329 at the stop beside the *Burger King*.
NOT IN SERVICE. NOT IN SERVICE.
The scraps of another discarded night
inundate the High Street outside Shopping City.
Sunday afternoon.
The peeling poster on the bottle-bank
beside *The Crown and Anchor*.
The Gotcha! cartoon, Thatcher
there in her noose.
Friday evening boozers fall
far short of yearned for yuppiedom
in *Drummond's* on the Euston Road.
A ragged man yanks a scarf
off a mannequin in Regent Street
and is away around a corner!
Rows of looted West-end shops,
like the remains of loud millionaires.

    Today it's swish book-stores,
magazines launching slick new issues,
literary associates and occasional friends
reading from latest collections.
Polite applause with murmurs of approval.
In this version the shadows somehow
having come to seem more tangible
than all that meaty stuff which had
the guts to cast them.

The Boy With No Face

I'm the boy with no face. My friends are all dead.
She wouldn't believe it was me. I won't run up, beam a hello.
   No.
I'll watch from a distance as she walks down the street,
free from jail at last. Mother. She never could cope anyway.
It's better this way.

I'm the boy with no face. It melted away as I dragged him free
from the blackening flames and the strangling fumes of the fire.
He was my friend you see.
If it wasn't for me he would have been dead,
there among the abandoned ashes of an empty building
where we cowered for one night to escape
the angry spit of the wind out of the cruel mouth
of another one of those invincible Russian winters.
Now he's dead anyway.

I'm the boy with no face.
I live in the damp basements and freezing cellars of humanity
scuttled away underneath St. Petersburg.
Pulverised walls eaten with mould threaten in on my space,
down among the stagnant smells, the rubbish and the rats,
on the bed I makeshifted from old pieces of cardboard.

I'm the boy with no face.
I wander at night, stand around the fires that blaze in the
   dead zones
at the stopped heart of this city. Casual acquaintances.
Sniff glue and petrol, learn to shoot up.

I'm the boy with no face. Too late for me now.
Sometime I'll be lost, the vicious night swirling
around my frayed edges, as I fade out under a MCDONALD's sign
and an ad for Demi Moore's latest film. STRIPTEASE.
Eleven years old. Oh yes, too late for me now.

Blackhole

This is the place where an old man with a twisted neck
falters on his way down a long pathway
to his privatised death in some musty, dark corner of a room.

This is the place where young men come out
into the shadows behind cemetery walls
to paint swastikas on headstones
and play football with skulls.

This is the place where council estates come complete
with built in big dogs and gunshots,
where a dull sun bakes the furnace air
as tower-block windows give that careless look
that only tranquillised eyes can throw,
where concrete thrusts pick the nose of the sky
as rubbish blows on the slow route to the paper heart of it all,
where the empty hours of the afternoon just get longer
      and longer,
where a drunk spunks out poison about Pakis and
      seven-year-olds
run junkie messages in Camelot House for carpet-knifed men
who carve reminders on the door,
where a wheel-chaired man belts the floor with his
      paranoid stick
and someone screams at a bare-knuckled wall
after the key-meter ran out,
where schizophrenics sit in timeless cafés
as matted hair women join pointless queues,
where a crack in the door shooter points up a bailiff nostril
as pools of liquid are in corners of the lift,
where police murders fall down stairs of convenience
and onto page nineteen,
where concealed Stanley-knives lurk
around scuttling cash-point machines

as lethal impressions hang
around the bus-shelter in the distance,
where asylum eyes poke out into the frantic spectre of the dusk
as endless discussions chase their tales
out through bizarre suicidal windows,
down to earth, where the dawn shines an angry light
into the bald face of the morning as nameless
blood stains another pavement,
where you could write slogans in the grime on the billboards
but no-one knows what to say now,
where arteries are clogged in North Circular bottlenecks
as ghettoblasters beat obscenities into the heads of grey
        old women,
where no-one asks the question
why do you write depressing poetry?

Here there are no nature walks,
no buttercups nor wild roses flourish.
No ripe autumn roads of blackberry brambles
bouncing along with a spring in their step.
Only poisoned grass by the railway.
Only grey-black slush dissolving the memory
of the last pure flake of snow.

This is the place where the city looks out through
        exhausted eyes,
where sweaty streets are all dressed up
in tasteless rectangular grey,
where day dreams flicker in café tea mugs
as cheapskate hotels rent out rooms by the hour.

This is the place,
just another sore in the mouth of the metropolis
where hope has been given an execution cigarette,
where it's very much a case of c'est la vie
as you straggle into the abyss of the echoing streets
at an insane hour after talking it all through.
This is the place from where no light escapes.

Lethargy

The pale yellow sun blinks
as it tries to shrug off the tiredness that grows,
when it's heard it all before.
This morning is jaded
like the faded print of last year's news.
The sky is lead heavy and splutters a cough.
The wind speaks in heavy-hearted whispers,
never rising to the occasion.
The tide has gone out and left a curt note,
that says it had enough
of hanging around for this charade.
Leaves on Avenue trees
droop low in dejection,
they know all is futile now.
The grass is thinning.
Flowers shrink and cower,
as their shades dull to blend
with the sameness all around.
The cat sits lazy on a garden wall,
where ivy grows in an aimless ramble,
as it waits for the autumn to pack it all in.